With the Light of Soul

A ramble through life

Aditi Chouhan

Introduction

I took it seriously when I heard channelling one's energy and converting weaknesses into strengths helps us grow. Being extremely enthusiastic about expressing everything I found interesting or thought-provoking I discussed it with people around me. Growing up, I understood that expressing it all in the written word is one of the best ways of sharing it with the world. Humans find solace in reading and it makes them think deeper than some conversations do.

I am very thankful for all the support given by my family and friends. I have immense gratitude in my heart for all the timely realizations I had in my life.

This book is a collection of quotes written by me. It will serve as your friend when you feel alone, it will also be a first step for the new readers.

Happy Reading :)

Aditi Chouhan

Lovers of monotony aren't ready for growth.

Aditi Chouhan

Passion comes with pain. I repeat, "Passion comes with pain".

Aditi Chouhan

"To do lists" always work, what does not work is your "will".

Aditi Chouhan

Timely realisations are the biggest gifts. Let us be grateful for them.

Aditi Chouhan

If you can trace back your past decisions, actions and choices and act after concluding atleast something from them, then and only then your experience matters.

Aditi Chouhan

If you say you're exhausted for yourself, forget
your dreams.

Aditi Chouhan

Some temporary solutions have the potential to become permanent blockers.

Aditi Chouhan

Metaphors used in life are momentary. Do not stick to them, if you do so, stagnancy will hinder your growth.

Aditi Chouhan

If it is making you restless, prioritize it and dive into it.

Aditi Chouhan

"What if" is the deadliest phrase unless you act. "What if" is the worst phrase without knowing the fact. "What if" is the best phrase if it begins to create reality out of abstract.

Aditi Chouhan

Heal before you leap.

Aditi Chouhan

Gossip is a weak expression by the weak.

Aditi Chouhan

"a No" (irrespective of its source) is not the end of the world...
...even though it is the most difficult thing to digest initially.

Aditi Chouhan

There can be no reason for saying NO but there can be a void resisting you to say YES. Decide wisely :)

Aditi Chouhan

A better fight. That's all for your goals.
(Inclusive of Wisdom)

Aditi Chouhan

Self control has always been the saviour of mankind in each and every era. Choose for yourself.

Aditi Chouhan

Of all the happiness in the world, one of the most special ones is when you over deliver.

Aditi Chouhan

It is the best when there is no need of reassurance.

Aditi Chouhan

And now that you realise how your parents were right in the first place, remember that there's a probability of your smart ways failing while explaining the same to your child. EXPERIENCES WORK, NOT WORDS even if the parental mind strives for precautions.

Aditi Chouhan

Each second when you are fighting with yourself, you are winning. Your self control is taking you up there.

Aditi Chouhan

Indecisiveness is human being's biggest enemy
as it leads to inaction and hence, stagnation.

Aditi Chouhan

Loop of monotony slaps the brain hard enough to make it dull.

Aditi Chouhan

It is a great feeling when there is no need of reassurance.

Aditi Chouhan

Do not link being straightforward with being a less loving person. Break it, it is a myth. The truth stands tall with love. IT DOES AND WILL ALWAYS.

Aditi Chouhan

An average mediocre mind thinks the most about society, sometimes the best or the worst, it thinks the deepest and wastes time enough to hamper growth and uses only enough to keep itself upto a certain standard, again mediocre. Let's Break The Loop!

Aditi Chouhan

Being able to answer only in a YES/NO is symbolic of Strength.

Aditi Chouhan

Those who're more interested in just knowing the future, have no right to blame the present.

Aditi Chouhan

A luxurious living space not maintained well is much uglier than a mediocre clean, arranged, maintained living space. The first spreads negativity, it speaks of an upcoming downfall though not so near but yes, coming. The later speaks of a thinking that has a potential to grow.

Aditi Chouhan

How deep you sink into it matters, not how much you read.

Aditi Chouhan

Do not make generalized statements when you're angry or just out of a disappointing conversation.

Aditi Chouhan

Ideologies, truths and concepts change a little bit when they pass through our individualities just like when light undergoes refraction but it still remains light.

Aditi Chouhan

Flexibility is the real flex.

Aditi Chouhan

Sometimes we need thirst and trust a little bit more than patience – to fail faster and not get left behind while being patient.

Aditi Chouhan

Humans are selfless only for their loved ones but that same action or behaviour is selfish for the outer world. The truth is: None of us is selfless completely. Otherwise we may become god!

Aditi Chouhan

We don't need people, we are co-dependent. When in love we want to do a lot for our beloved people and that is why we become co-dependent. People stay for either of the reasons love or co-dependency. And the relationship survives.

Aditi Chouhan

Sometimes one should recall the time when something or someone entered our life, how happy we were to have them...only then we remember their value and make efforts to keep it all good. Because not having them was not as good as having them.

Aditi Chouhan

Discuss but do not gossip.
Think but not people.
Serve but do not expect.
Expect but not from people.

Aditi Chouhan

We talk about waking up on time BUT bathing and combing your hair on time also makes your day 100x better.

Aditi Chouhan

Life can be good and we can still work on its quality.

Aditi Chouhan

Over analysis changes destiny.

Aditi Chouhan

Human beings love to and they always EXPECT. They fool themselves by distracting themselves to believe that they do not expect. As long as the self fooling game is strong, they think they're okay.

Aditi Chouhan

Life can never be on autopilot, it will always be driven by our Karma even if we stop putting any efforts. The only way to come out of old karmic web is trying your best at everything in ethical ways.

Aditi Chouhan

When perception deceives, trust your eyesight. It happens when it's known by people and you listen to it quite often, in these cases it may turn the tables against you unconsciously.

Aditi Chouhan

Revisiting realisations is important. Renewing the feeling that would make you keep walking in the right direction is important.

Aditi Chouhan

Off the track but on the way – trust the process when awareness is in your basic nature.

Aditi Chouhan

Trust the logic you just built in your brain enough to try it, otherwise you may not end up how and where you wanted to be.

Aditi Chouhan

Very less people dare to think deeper that requires tiring the brain. Probably this is the reason, very few come up with unique ideas and very few people code well. Should we call it mental laziness?

Aditi Chouhan

Your self talk determines your success or failure more than anything else.

Aditi Chouhan

Control your thoughts while cooking, what you think is what you'll eat.

Aditi Chouhan

Life is so much about how simple, compound or complex sentences you speak with others and with yourself. The nature of the verbal communication affects the brain and thinking patterns in different ways.

Aditi Chouhan

The one who takes the first step keeps on
marching ahead.
The one with the reason keeps on reasoning.
The one who does both truly tries to balance
and often emerges victorious.

Aditi Chouhan

If you let the pieces out of your mind on the paper and try to solve the puzzle the solution will definitely pay you peace.

Aditi Chouhan

Disciplined thought process shouldn't sound unachievable in the presence of self control and seriousness for your dreams. They are its core components. Read it again only if you want to grow.

Aditi Chouhan

Beating anticipation is a way to beat procrastination.

Aditi Chouhan

Freedom can help creativity but the art and inventions done by the prisoners, the slaves, the underprivileged and the desperate; prove that creativity is about being able to find the best way out in any given condition.

Aditi Chouhan

When you have no reason to expect but you find yourself expecting, understand that your heart is ruling over your head. Give the charge back to your brain to avoid hurting yourself.

Aditi Chouhan

Raw is Real.
Raw is Pure.
Raw is Brave.
But decide if it's situationally useful or not.

Aditi Chouhan

The vague and baseless reasons of not executing New Ideas or adapting to New Ways drown you so slowly that you do not realize it until you can't breathe

Aditi Chouhan

When you want to spend less time getting ready and looking presentable, you have to work on the basics like skin care and hair care daily, you need to plan what you need to wear. Now, if you say you have less time for all of this then better be aware that you are being consumed by some external forces for example your phone or anything inside. Time wasted is time lost. If your things aren't streamlined you are definitely going to fall down a little more every day and write a destiny of misery and slavery for yourself. The more you respect yourself, the happier will be your life. LIFE BASICS affect the quality of life. This is not just about external things but this is all connected to the depths of you.

Aditi Chouhan

Diversify but prioritize, analyze and then prioritize. Prioritize and then trust the process.

Aditi Chouhan

Process your guilt before it eats you up.
Channelize it or simply get distracted from in
order to stop yourself from overthinking.

Aditi Chouhan

Initially, when you start finding clarity in your thoughts and the related situations, you will feel proud of yourself, it takes time but we definitely land in a place where we learn to seek clarity from other perspectives too, only then do we understand the meaning of different perspectives and intentions in the true sense.

Aditi Chouhan

Success is decided the moment you fail, because only the mindset that is wired for winning will not give up and learn from failures.

Aditi Chouhan

Every random thought in your mind that takes you to a completely different topic shows you the potential of your thinking capacity and your set style of thinking. If you look at it closely and observe any continuous patterns and you like them, never stop. I do not encourage deviation but I promote the analysis of the thought chain. Apply your patterns anywhere you believe they will bring you profits ethically.

Aditi Chouhan

Luxury varies but one kind that is the same for the people of every financial group is nothing but scooping out some time just by being disciplined. This luxury can be used to achieve any kind of goal.

Aditi Chouhan

Building, maintaining, updating, retiring generators of any kind generates more money than the one time generation result. It builds you wealth.

Aditi Chouhan

Being desparate is a catalyst for a great project. What makes you desparate might feel like a curse but it leads you to the foundation of something great, very brave of me to say this. Let your actions be morally correct.

Aditi Chouhan

It is an important task to set the visibility of your potential to specific groups of people. If it gets sensed by the wrong ones, you get depleted by them just like resources get.

Aditi Chouhan

Warnings received sound like a lack of trust in them to the receiver whereas the full trust in the giver's experience is the real thing which again is not wrong for the receiver.

Aditi Chouhan

Humans learn life lessons while building artificial intelligence because only then do they know how valuable is sharing of experience is and how the finished product should be errorless.

Aditi Chouhan

A good software developer will never let technical debts be a part of his work, this attitude makes them win. Or the foresightedness makes them a good developer. Be it anything but at last everything comes to discipline and integrity.

Aditi Chouhan

Tone and words can make or break, bring the power of self control and wisdom into the play.

Aditi Chouhan

Making your own thoughts clear and streamlined can act as great tools but don't let them become rigid walls.

Aditi Chouhan

Guilt arising out of you considering someone a wrong person eats you up, better not anticipate or speak about them unless known well.

Aditi Chouhan

Basic dependency – This exists without any judgments only when there is a bond or a genuine interest in the formation of a bond or it is the part of a deal. It is removed again in the same cases, but out of these cases all others are called favours that are not always compeltely comfort giving to both the sides.

Aditi Chouhan

Most of the wisdom is proven with actions after the results not just by stating analogies and metaphors in simple languages.

Aditi Chouhan

Questioning the existence and root of the question is not always right or wrong. It depends on us how we want it to end.

Aditi Chouhan

It is brave to pick a side which is also wise. The fearful wears a mask of wisdom and says that they are not in a condition or position to pick any of the sides. To be brave, be knowledgeable and ethical.

Aditi Chouhan

The intersection of law and what means right to you will not be a common/frequent happening in your mind. Before going through a tough journey to arrive at this intersection, learn from observation.

Aditi Chouhan

Fun measured is the right way to live, it drives you towards the balance the whole world is seeking.

Aditi Chouhan

Because we analyse only the problems, we master the blame game and keep getting more of them. The day you analyze success, you will get more of it. None of them can be ignored, biased analysis welcomes an unforeseen trouble disguised as perfection.

Aditi Chouhan

Being less attentive does not mean fun and peace.

Aditi Chouhan

Escape and freedom from an issue are not to be confused. Escape is never ending whereas freedom is the feeling after facing the problem successfully irrespective of the result.

Aditi Chouhan

Freedom comes into two parts – initially you can celebrate it and later you plan to grow. People who forget the second part still remain in the clutches of their own attitude that might slowly poison them and are actually not free.

Aditi Chouhan

Freedom is not the end it is the state and conditions you get into that have immense potential for growth.

Aditi Chouhan

Escape is nothing but procrastination in dealing with something that needs you to come out of your comfort zone.

Aditi Chouhan

Being a little kind to someone else's feelings and making a jinx-proof shield for yourself both includes timely and conscious announcements and not just a free flow of news and expressions AND a check of what kind of person the listener is, harsh truth to be gulped.

Aditi Chouhan

Brutal honesty is a sharp knife that creates no mess. It sometimes needs to be dressed well only to be accepted with open arms because how you approach while speaking, matters a lot.

Aditi Chouhan

You cannot pay for peace, it has to be created.

Aditi Chouhan

Reassurance is important everywhere but the right interval and following actions needs to be managed.

Aditi Chouhan

Being only a consumer will lose you your respect.

Aditi Chouhan

It is not about what teaches you, the real game changer is what makes you think and act.

Aditi Chouhan

If the only focus is on "what needs to be done" and "what you want to or have to do" is ignored, one cannot surpass mediocrity be it career or relationships.

Aditi Chouhan

Relationships do not work only with understanding, you need to do something, then only there will be something to be understood. Otherwise, just staying in a relationship and seeing each other's life unfold will not feed the bond. The bonds too need to be fed with actions.

Aditi Chouhan

94

Staying for someone has different meanings everytime according to the situation. If we stick to just one, the whole existense of the relation becomes meaningless.

Aditi Chouhan

Under-commitment has its benefits but make sure it does not make you sound rude, less of what you are expected to be and become a cause for breaking instead of building trust. Over-delivery later will help you elevate yourself.

Aditi Chouhan

It is about you, how and when you want to do it. The last-moment pressure that works for some people very well is equal to the enthusiasm and the will that other people have, the ones who complete things on time.

Aditi Chouhan

Revision is not just limited to students and studies, it comes into play each time when we need to get back on track without neglecting our moral values. Being an avid reader, and observer and taking breaks to analyse situations and changing perspectives helps us revise the ultimate truths and values that keep us rooted in ethics.

Aditi Chouhan

Silence and loudness both have reasons, sudden emergence of any of the two is a matter of concern but not panic, panic usually spoils everything.

Aditi Chouhan

The most unfortunate is the one who ignores his own awareness.

Aditi Chouhan

Controlling the urge to gossip and eat junk sorts your life issues to a huge extent.

Aditi Chouhan

Wise challenges, weird "what ifs", will power –
three things that support invention

Aditi Chouhan

Expect things to come unordered in life, make yourself strong enough to not lose it when complex issues pop up together and abrupt changes occur.

Aditi Chouhan

Our brain needs to be trained but not conditioned.

Aditi Chouhan

If you have a lot on your plate, learn how to co-relate only then you will understand the importance of having variety. This applies to many aspects of our life.

Aditi Chouhan

Assumptions, misunderstandings, unnecesarry reactions, arguments – the foundations of a shaky relationship

Aditi Chouhan

Not being verbally voilent is not a virtue but basic humanity,

Aditi Chouhan

The way evolution is noticed only when a stage is reached, self-development is also noticed in the same way. Many self-developed people collectively make evolution happen. So, why do we in the 2020s want to not evolve?

Aditi Chouhan

Denial of trial in absence of risk factors – this attitude is quite predictive of mediocrity.

Aditi Chouhan

Some parts of communication have an expiry,
prioritize accordingly.

Aditi Chouhan

Lack of self confidence and insecurities give birth to Selfishness.

Aditi Chouhan

The trigger to be grateful will never come when we need it and it is not always a positive situation, we need to be aware of our privileges and luxuries (not just of the material kind).

Aditi Chouhan

Sensitivity is a strength when used correctly will help you win every battle of life.

Aditi Chouhan

113

Emotional intelligence is born out of sensitivity only and the higher this intelligence, the higher degree of moral value strength is needed to keep our Karma on the right track.

Aditi Chouhan

Becoming the best never hurts but when you go through the process nobody should be hurt.

Aditi Chouhan

Self defence to conceal under-performance is like slow poison for yourself.

Aditi Chouhan

Nobody deserves your forgiveness everytime for their lack of punctuality, if you do not agree with this, you will see your value degrade.

Aditi Chouhan

Picking up your own pieces has to be done by yourself, people can be just temporary supports.

Aditi Chouhan

Never state the obvious things that imply that you are not close to the person, that pricks people in the heart, they know it and are at peace with it, just don't speak that.

Aditi Chouhan

Check what the fun costs you, if you have no idea of how to have it without money, you need to re-learn what fun is.

Aditi Chouhan

Apropos of habit cultivation, it should be done for a purpose and not because of your financial condition.

Aditi Chouhan

Your honesty holds the power to turn the tables,
it just needs patience and a keen eye of
observation to pick the time.

Aditi Chouhan

You can't quantify your love and neither can you get qualified as a great lover until your actions and support confirm it irrespective of the situations you and your partner face.

Aditi Chouhan

Learn to take care of a plant and keep it alive before you start a family.

Aditi Chouhan

The Extra and the Boundary - only two things
if understood can blossom the relationships.
Because only the basics OR anything
too much... spoils.

Aditi Chouhan

The city that is young will need you and the city that is grown up will also need you. Why? Because the buds are loved always and paid attention to AND when the bloom they are always in demand.

Aditi Chouhan

There is no harm in being the lighthouse but there is guilt after ignorance of some events of which people around you are a part.

Aditi Chouhan

Responsibility is not a weight but an important catalyser for our growth even if disguised a difficulty initially.

Aditi Chouhan

The feeling of ownership brings responsibility, otherwise it is all casual and linient. Own to grow.

Aditi Chouhan

If the idea of doing it 'now' does not excite you,
it is not for you.

Aditi Chouhan

Initiative is medicine against monotony, initiative needs courage. Hence, courage can only break monotony.

Aditi Chouhan

Poetry is not an escape from the reality, poetry is the depiction of the deepest realities in the most beautiful ways. The company of poems will not make you lazy, your own viewpoints might.

Aditi Chouhan

Excitement when holds hands with Endurance to reach a goal, the alliance can break world records.

Aditi Chouhan

Forgiveness is a difficult to reach destination, it comes with time and wisdom; it blesses you with immense peace. The road might be tricky as many of the turns remind you of the past and your feelings.

Aditi Chouhan

Preachy attitude repels people from you. Accepting attitude can make you many friends but it might also make people take you for granted. Not letting your attitude get learnt by people will keep you safe.

Aditi Chouhan

Reading people is an art they say, it is a shield they say. I say that, not everyone is great at art and not everyone has the privilege of a shield, some of us just know enough to be on the track and protect ourselves, if this is okay for survival, we are not lacking anything as long as we are pure.

Aditi Chouhan

Normalising the not so normal is a wave that hits the mankind in every century and years later regrets dressed as fresh realizations become the fashion again. Loop and reality of the human world it is! Those who stick to the basics are the winners, ever growing and strong like the Banyan tree.

Aditi Chouhan

The probability of winning lies in your capacity to imagine the desired state. If you can't imagine, your belief will not be set on your actions which will lead to decisions that might shake the whole idea.

Aditi Chouhan

Falling in love is like integration in action that finds area of an irregular shape. Because doesn't falling in love start small? Initially finite reasons and later difficult to define and large. It's all the little things added together. Remember there are real boundaries and limits too.

Aditi Chouhan

Similarity generates likeability because of familiarity and an undiscovered yet existing self love.

Aditi Chouhan

People may smell like Trust or Wisdom. It takes us time to understand that it is not always a Fragrance.

Aditi Chouhan

Like flowers, you too can be seasonal, but only when you water yourself regularly, you will bloom.

Aditi Chouhan

Before your disinterest shows up, drop the job
or try that you don't spoil it.

Aditi Chouhan

Everyone thinks that the judgements should be based on their strengths. If that was the case, they would've won. But nobody thinks to increase their strengths.

Aditi Chouhan

More than our loved ones need to hear, "I believe you will do it" they need to hear "I am by your side without judging the outcomes because I know you give your best". They aslo need to hear the real things. Love cannot always sound positive. Love cannot always be criticising but it can be an honest critic, it is not about mocking in public. Love will always choose the right thing to be heard by the beloved.

Aditi Chouhan

For every unborn thought, we pay a price. For every condition that aborted the thought, we ourselves are responsible or to be blamed. In every blame game, we are the only losers. Again, we arent't the centre of our destiny but our rigidity, our resistance to change of state is (in any aspect) is.

Aditi Chouhan

The quest of getting more is never ending but the project of creating more is often procrastinated or feared of.

Aditi Chouhan

An effort goes a long way, if it doesn't, redirect it darling!

Aditi Chouhan

Acceptance and the thoughts followed by make
all the difference.

Aditi Chouhan

149

How much you reveal decides the quality of your life.

Aditi Chouhan

When emotional needs of two people get fulfilled naturally by each other that feeling is the beginning of true love. That comfort is true love. You won't find insecurities there.

Aditi Chouhan

Saying is not promising but just doing what you say makes your promises trustworthy.

Aditi Chouhan

Whatever you find the most difficult to speak, if spoken has the potential to make your life easier, lighter and happier.

Aditi Chouhan

Love co-exists with many emotions. Sometimes, those emotions give rise to love and sometimes it is vice versa but life is all about finding a balance between them all.

Aditi Chouhan

Life is all about Dreams vs Desperate Choices. The only way of making dreams come true is to avoid creating situations where you have to make any desperate choices.

Aditi Chouhan

Hate is what degrades humanity. Love is what acquaints us of our capabilities.

Aditi Chouhan

Expectations are born with the human. The proof is the cry for the breast milk for the second time.

Aditi Chouhan

Illusions are also a discovery. A discovery before the discovery that quenches the thirst called curiosity.

Aditi Chouhan

Getting a critic and the one who celebrates you the most, in the same person is a blessing.

Aditi Chouhan

The soul needs to be strong to consume the facts raw.

Aditi Chouhan

Your choices are the most honest you.

Aditi Chouhan

www.ingramcontent.com/pod-product-compliance
Lightning Source LLC
Chambersburg PA
CBHW021402150726
47989CB00005B/2365